A HISTORICAL ALBUM OF
OHIO

A HISTORICAL ALBUM OF

OHIO

Charles A. Wills

THE MILLBROOK PRESS, Brookfield, Connecticut

*Front and back cover: "Cleveland Public Square." Painting by Sebastian Heine, 1839.
Western Reserve Historical Society, Cleveland, Ohio.*

*Title page: Glen Helen. Photograph by Terry Cartwright. Courtesy of the
Ohio Division of Travel and Tourism.*

Library of Congress Cataloging-in-Publication Data

Wills, Charles A.
    A historical album of Ohio / Charles A. Wills.
       p. cm. – (Historical Albums)
    Includes bibliographical references and index.
    Summary: A history of Ohio, from its early exploration and
settlement to the state today.
    ISBN 1-56294-593-9 (lib. bdg.)   ISBN 0-7613-0086-4 (tr. pbk.)
    1. Ohio—History—Juvenile literature. 2. Ohio—
Gazetteers—Juvenile literature. I. Title. II. Series.
F491.3.W55 1996
977.1—dc20   95-40421
                                          CIP
                                          AC

 Created in association with Media Projects Incorporated

    C. Carter Smith, *Executive Editor*
    Kimberly Horstman, *Project Editor*
    Charles A. Wills, *Principal Writer*
    Bernard Schleifer, *Art Director*
    John W. Kern, *Production Editor*
    Arlene Goldberg, *Cartographer*

    Consultant: Nancy Taylor, classroom teacher, St. Michael School,
Worthington, Ohio, Ohio Historical Society children's program
consultant, and National Council for History Education elementary mentor

Manufactured in the United States of America

10 9 8 7 6 5 4 3 2

CONTENTS

Introduction

In the words of writer Louis Bromfield, "Ohio is the farthest west of the East and the farthest north of the South."

Today, most Americans tend to look at Ohio as a typical northeastern state—a land of big cities and sprawling suburbs, densely populated and filled with industry. As Bromfield pointed out, however, Ohio was once the beginning of the western frontier. When Americans started heading west after the Revolutionary War, many went to the Ohio Country, as it was then called, to start a new life.

The abundance of land in Ohio lured settlers from both New England and the South, and over the next two centuries the state's thriving economy, excellent location, and rich natural resources attracted waves of newcomers from both overseas and the rest of the nation. Thus, Ohio's human history is one of the richest and most diverse of all the states.

From the time it achieved statehood in 1803, it took only a few decades for Ohio to become one of America's wealthiest and most populous states. Along the way, Ohio has given the nation eight presidents, a small army of notable politicians, businesspeople, soldiers, and scientists, in addition to many individuals who have left significant marks on American history—from the Wright brothers to Neil Armstrong.

Today, modern Ohio, a state in America's heartland, struggles to keep up with changing times, yet it remains at the heart of the American experience.

PART ONE

THE LAND OF THE BEAUTIFUL RIVER

A steamboat passes Cleveland Lighthouse in this 19th-century painting by Karl Bodmer. Cleveland's location at the point where the Cuyahoga River meets Lake Erie made the city an important port from its founding.

The land that is now Ohio was home to several Native American cultures, including the great Mound Builders, before the first French explorers arrived in the region in the late 1600s. Claimed by both France and Britain, Ohio came under U.S. rule following the Revolutionary War as part of the Northwest Territory. Marietta, the first white settlement in Ohio, was founded in 1788, and despite resistance from the region's Native Americans, Ohio grew so rapidly that it achieved statehood only fifteen years later. After the War of 1812, Ohio's population continued to rise, and by the middle of the 19th century the state was an agricultural and industrial powerhouse.

Ohio's Earliest Peoples

About 25,000 years ago, at the end of the last Ice Age, a river of ice called the Wisconsian Glacier covered much of the land that is now the state of Ohio. Huge animals called mastodons and mammoths (much like elephants) roamed in the ice-free areas of the region. These animals were hunted by the first settlers known to have reached Ohio—an ancient people who archaeologists (scientists who study the material remains of the distant past) have named the Paleo Indians.

The Paleo Indians were nomadic hunters who moved from place to place following the animals they hunted for food. Archaeologists have found some of the stone tools and weapons these early hunters used. From this ancient evidence they have shown that the Paleo Indians lived in Ohio as early as 20,000 B.C.

Over time, however, the big game disappeared—some believe herds simply migrated northward following the slow-moving glaciers, while others believe that the Paleo Indians overhunted the mammoths and mastodons and they eventually became extinct. As a result, the Paleo Indians no longer had these animals to hunt, a fact that may have led to that culture's demise.

When glaciers no longer covered Ohio's landscape, the land emerged as a region of fertile soil, lush forests, and important waterways—especially the mighty Ohio River, which today forms the state's southern border. The Ohio connects with the Mississippi River system and thus is a gateway to both the interior of North America and to the Gulf of Mexico. The river also gave the present state its name: Native Americans called the waterway Oheo, which probably meant "great river" or "beautiful river."

The next group of people to settle in Ohio were known as the Archaic Peoples. What distinguished this group from the Paleo Indians was a more varied diet. The Archaic Peoples hunted smaller game, like bear, deer, and turkey, with flint-tipped spears, and fished in lakes and rivers. They also ate nuts, berries, roots, and other wild plant foods and may have farmed squash and other crops.

The Archaic Peoples developed a wide range of tools, including axes and cooking utensils made from materials such as stone, wood, bone, antler, and shell. In addition, they were the first people to weave plant materials into baskets and sandals. While they didn't live in permanent villages, they did bury their dead in *kames*, mounds of earth formed by the movement of glaciers. Succeeding cultures in the Ohio region would greatly expand this tradition.

The next major culture to develop arrived in the area about 2,000 years ago. This culture was made up of several groups that are known collectively as the Mound Builders because of the monuments they left behind.

The Mound Builders—especially the Hopewell Peoples, who flourished 1,500 years ago—created an amazingly sophisticated civilization in the Ohio River Valley. Aside from hunting, gathering, and farming, they established far-ranging trade routes that stretched east to the Atlantic Coast, west to the Rocky Mountains, and south to the Gulf of Mexico.

Excellent planners and builders, the Mound Builders left behind Ohio's famous burial and ceremonial mounds. Villages usually centered around these earth mounds, which covered as much as 100 acres and sometimes rose to heights of more than 60 feet. They were often cone-shaped, although some mounds were inspired by natural shapes. The best-known mound to have survived into our own time, the Great Serpent Mound in Adams County, is in the form of a giant snake and stretches nearly 1,300 feet.

For reasons that are still not understood, the Mound Builder civilization fell into decline and decay around A.D. 600. Changes in climate, war with other tribes, or a disease epidemic may have led to the collapse of the Hopewell Culture. At the same time, however, another mound-building culture, the Mississippian Peoples, emerged to take their place. The Mississippians, like similar civilizations in

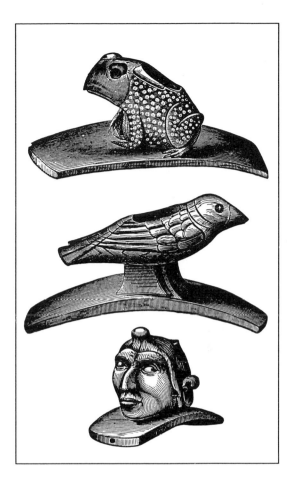

The skill of the Mound Builders can be seen in these carved effigy pipes, found preserved in an Ohio mound. Countless artifacts of the Mound Builder civilization, however, were probably broken into pieces by pioneer farmers plowing their fields.

Mexico and Central America, built pyramid-shaped mounds. But over time they, too, disappeared from the region.

Several Native American groups migrated into Ohio toward the end of the 17th century. Some of these groups were fleeing the warriors of the Iroquois Confederacy, a powerful league of five Native American nations based in present-day New York.

The Iroquois began their drive westward by wiping out the Eries, a tribe living on the southern shore of Lake Erie, in the 1650s. Using guns obtained from European traders, the Iroquois were unbeatable, and they steadily pushed weaker tribes westward into the Ohio region. Deadly and unfamiliar diseases like smallpox, also brought by contact with Europeans, killed whole Native American villages and aided the Iroquois in their campaigns.

Among the new arrivals in Ohio were the Leni Lenapes, or Delawares, whom the Iroquois forced out of what is now Pennsylvania; the Wyandots (also known as the Hurons) and the Ottawas, who came to Ohio from Canada; and the Miamis and Shawnees, who migrated into Ohio from the south and west and joined together to become the region's most powerful Native American group.

By the early 1700s, nearly 15,000 Native Americans lived in the Ohio Country. These Native Americans found the region a land of plenty—corn grew high in rich soil, forests were filled with game, and rivers, lakes, and streams teemed with fish and waterfowl. Their villages flourished—until European trappers and traders discovered the riches of the Ohio Country.

This photograph shows an aerial view of the Great Serpent Mound, built by the Adena Peoples sometime between 800 B.C. and A.D. 400. In 1888, Ohio's state legislature passed a law protecting this and other important archaeological sites from development.

International Rivalry

During the 17th century, England established a string of colonies along North America's Atlantic Coast while a rival nation, France, took the lead in exploring and settling present-day Canada. From Canadian bases, French explorers and traders moved into the wilderness south of the Great Lakes and along the Mississippi River.

These hardy Frenchmen were less interested in setting up permanent settlements than in trading with the Native Americans for furs, which fetched high prices in the markets of Europe. Along with them went Roman Catholic missionaries, many of them members of the Jesuit religious order, who were eager to convert the Native Americans to Christianity.

The first Frenchman (and probably the first European) to set foot in present-day Ohio was Robert Cavalier, Sieur de La Salle, who journeyed through the region in 1669–70. La Salle's exploration was the foundation for France's claim to the area. It isn't known if La Salle reached the Ohio River, but by the mid-1670s maps published in France clearly showed the great waterway.

The French claim to the Ohio River Valley was soon challenged by the English. The English colonists on the Atlantic Coast believed their land extended westward into the area claimed by France, and they too were interested in reaping the rich profits of the fur trade. In the late 1600s, traders from New York, Virginia, Pennsylvania, and other colonies pushed west across the Appalachian Mountains and south from Lake Erie into the Ohio River Valley.

The region's Native Americans became caught in the middle of a

Shown here is Robert Cavalier, Sieur de La Salle. Much remains unknown about the explorer's 1669–70 journey into the Ohio Country. Historians once credited him with reaching the Ohio River, but today it is believed that he merely heard about the great river from the Native Americans he encountered.

struggle between France and England for power in the rich Ohio Country. Each side sought to win the loyalty—and the furs—of the Native American nations with offerings of trade goods such as guns, tools, and alcohol. The British and French also formed military alliances that set Native American nations against one another to win control of territory. The British were supported by the powerful Iroquois Confederacy and the Miami Indians, while the French had the aid of the Hurons, a longtime enemy of the Iroquois, and many smaller Native American nations.

To firm up their control of the Ohio Country, the French built outposts on the shores of Lake Erie and on the Maumee and Muskingum rivers, in the early 1700s. In 1749, in a further effort to keep the English out of the region, a French officer named Pierre-Joseph Céleron de Bienville buried lead plates along the Ohio River. These "markers," engraved with the date, location, and a statement of France's claim to the area, warned the British to keep out.

The British didn't. Growing numbers of traders were doing business in the Ohio Country, and some colonists began to see the region as a favorable land for settlement. At the same time Céleron de Bienville was planting his plates, a group of Virginians formed the Ohio Company. The British government granted the company's investors 200,000 acres of land along

The growing European presence in the Ohio Country can be seen in this engraving from a book published in Italy in the mid-1700s: Native Americans armed with muskets shoot beavers for their valuable pelts, probably in the hopes of exchanging the furs with British and French traders for more guns and tools.

the Ohio River; in return, the company agreed to settle a certain number of families in the region.

In 1750, the company sent out explorer Christopher Gist to survey (determine the boundaries of) its holdings. Almost two years and 1,200 miles later, Gist returned with a glowing report: "The Ohio Country is fine, rich, level land, well timbered. . . . In

In these engravings, French (left) and British (right) soldiers are shown carrying the equipment and wearing the uniforms common at the time of the French and Indian War.

short, it wants nothing but cultivation to make it a most delightful country."

In the 1750s the tensions between Britain and France heated up, and as always the Native Americans were caught in the middle. Both nations wanted the loyalty of the main Miami chief, called Old Briton by the British and La Demoiselle by the French. Old Briton decided to side with the British and paid for this loyalty with his life. In June 1750, a party of Frenchmen and their Native American allies attacked the largest Miami village, Pickawillany, while most of the British soldiers were off hunting. Outnumbered, Old Briton and many of his warriors were killed and the village was destroyed.

Four years later a young Virginian named George Washington arrived in the wilderness with orders to build a fort to protect the Ohio Country from the French. French troops captured the outpost, Fort Necessity, in an episode that helped touch off the great conflict known in Europe as the Seven Years War and in America as the French and Indian War. Britain was the victor, and in a 1763 peace treaty France gave up its claim to the Ohio Country.

Settling the Ohio Country

The end of the French and Indian War didn't end conflict in the Ohio Country. In order to keep peace with the region's Native Americans, the British government forbade its American colonists from settling west of the Ohio River. The law was widely ignored, however, and as white settlers moved into the Ohio Country, the Native Americans became increasingly angry.

In 1763, warriors from Native American nations across the country joined together under the leadership of the Ottawa chief Pontiac to drive white settlers from their homeland. It took an army of more than 1,000 men to put down what the whites called Pontiac's Rebellion.

Fighting between whites and Native Americans flared up again in the mid-1770s, leading Lord Dunmore, governor of Virginia, to send an army of colonists into the Ohio Country. The conflict ended when the Virginians defeated Shawnee chief Cornstalk and his warriors.

Both Pontiac's Rebellion and Lord Dunmore's War were bitter conflicts, with massacres and cruelties on each side. But during these years a remarkable group of people proved that Native Americans and white settlers could live together peacefully in the Ohio Country—for a time, at least.

These people were Moravians, members of a pacifist Christian group who had come originally from what is now the Czech Republic and settled in Pennsylvania in large numbers.

The Delawares had known and respected the Moravians since the days when both groups lived in Pennsylvania. Now settled in the Ohio Country, the Delawares invited Moravian missionaries to come and live among them. In the early 1770s, Moravians

Based on a painting by Benjamin West, this engraving shows the October 1764 meeting between Pontiac and Colonel Henry Bouquet, the British officer who commanded the forces sent to put down the Native American "rebellion" on the Great Lakes frontier. Pontiac was later murdered in mysterious circumstances.

Native Americans of the Leni Lenape nation listen to a sermon preached by a Moravian missionary. The Moravian missionary schools established for Native American children were the first educational institutions in Ohio.

founded several villages along the Tuscarawas and Muskingum rivers.

In the mid-1770s, however, the Ohio Country's Native Americans again had to choose sides in a conflict between whites. This time the conflict was between Britain and the American colonists who wanted independence—a conflict known as the Revolutionary War. Because the British had tried to prevent American settlers from taking over the Native Americans' land, most tribes either stayed neutral or sided with the British. Throughout the war, Native Americans raided the handful of white settlements on the Ohio frontier.

The bloodiest incident of the Revolutionary War in the Ohio Country came in the conflict's last years. The Delawares and the Moravian mission-aries had stuck to their peaceful principles and refused to become entangled in the war. This angered both the British, who killed several Moravian missionaries in 1781, and the Americans, who were guilty of a much bloodier outrage a year later, when nearly 100 Delawares were slaughtered at the village of Gnadenhutten. News of this massacre set off another wave of Native American attacks in the Ohio Country.

In 1783 the Revolutionary War ended with a peace treaty that gave the Americans independence from

Britain and fixed the new nation's western border at the Mississippi River. Thus, the Ohio Country was finally open to American settlers.

Before such settlement could begin in earnest, however, several important issues had to be resolved. Some had to do with who "owned" the land west of the Ohio River. Several of the new states, for example, claimed huge stretches of western land on the basis of old colonial claims.

There were also challenging political issues. How were the new lands to be organized and governed? Would they one day become states in their own right, or would they be colonies of the original thirteen states?

The ownership issue was resolved by compromises between state governments and the national government. Virginia and Connecticut, the states with the biggest land claims, agreed to let the federal government control the region. In return, both states received huge grants of land for their citizens to settle on. Connecticut received its Western Reserve of more than 3 million acres in northern Ohio, while the Virginia Military District to the south covered more than 4 million acres. (The military district got its name from the fact that Virginia granted much of this land to Revolutionary War veterans.)

The political issues were resolved in the Northwest Ordinance of 1787, one of the most important documents in American history. The ordinance

This map, which shows the United States after the Revolutionary War, indicates the land claims of the various states in the Northwest Territory. Besides Ohio, four other states were eventually created from the vast territory—Indiana, Illinois, Michigan, and Wisconsin.

organized the entire Great Lakes region, including the Ohio Country, into the Northwest Territory. It established rules for admitting parts of the territory to the Union as states, on an equal basis with the original states, once their populations had reached a certain number; guaranteed free speech and trial by jury; lent public support of education; and outlawed slavery in the territory.

From Frontier to Statehood

The Ohio Country's rise to statehood began in 1786 in a Boston tavern called The Bunch of Grapes. It was there that several businessmen formed a company to buy land in the Ohio Country on which New England families could settle.

The firm these men set up became known as the Ohio Company of Associates, or the Second Ohio Company, to distinguish it from the earlier Ohio Company of Virginia. Under the energetic leadership of Moses Cleaveland and Rufus Putnam, the company bought 1.5 million acres of Ohio land from the government and advertised across New England for settlers.

In the spring of 1788, the first party of pioneers set out for the Ohio Country. Forty-eight men (their wives and children would come later) made the overland journey across Pennsylvania and then floated down the Ohio River in a fifty-ton flatboat named *The Adventure Gallery.*

At the junction of the Ohio and Muskingum rivers the settlers built a fort for protection from the Native Americans and cabins for the women and children, who arrived two months

Shown here is Marietta, the first American settlement in Ohio, as it looked in the early 1800s. The large building in the foreground is the Washington County courthouse, built in 1798, ten years after the settlement was founded. Its shingle-and-clapboard construction reflects the New England heritage of the early Ohio pioneers.

later. The New Englanders named their settlement Marietta, after Marie Antoinette, Queen of France, to thank that nation for helping the American cause during the Revolutionary War. The forty-eight pioneers at Marietta were the first of about 10,000 people, most New Englanders, who migrated to the Ohio Country between 1788 and 1790.

General Arthur St. Clair, governor of the Northwest Territory, chose the settlement at Losantiville as the territory's capital in 1788. He changed Losantiville's name to Cincinnati in 1790 to honor the Society of the Cincinnati, an organization of Revolutionary War veterans.

Both white settlers and Native Americans knew it was only a matter of time before fighting broke out between the two groups. Native American nations throughout the region were unwilling to stand by while ever-growing numbers of white settlers invaded their homelands. "The idea of being ultimately obliged to abandon their country," wrote St. Clair, "rankles in their minds."

Attacks on white settlements increased in 1790, leading George Washington, now president of the United States, to order military action against the Native Americans on the northwest frontier.

In the beginning things went badly for the Americans. In 1790, General Josiah Harmar led a ragtag army of frontiersmen against the warriors of the Miami, Ojibwa, Potawatomi, and Shawnee nations, united under the able leadership of Little Turtle, a Miami chief. Little Turtle's warriors easily defeated Harmar and his men.

Encouraged by this victory, Native American war parties rampaged up and down the Ohio frontier, burning settlements and killing or taking settlers captive. In 1791, 2,000 American soldiers commanded by St. Clair marched against Little Turtle and his warriors. Little Turtle set an ambush and the Americans blundered into it. About 900 soldiers were killed and the rest, including St. Clair, were forced into a headlong retreat.

In desperation, Washington turned to one of his most able Revolutionary War commanders—General Anthony Wayne. Instead of rushing into battle like Harmar and St. Clair, Wayne spent a year training a fighting force that could match the Native Americans.

Throughout the summer of 1794, Wayne's troops skirmished with Native Americans and built forts deep within the Ohio Country. Then, in August, Wayne found the chance he was looking for—a thousand Native American warriors camped along the Maumee River. A recent storm had felled many trees along the riverbank, so the August 20 battle fought there came to be known as the Battle of Fallen Timbers. The fight lasted less than an hour, and when it ended the Native Americans were in retreat. The Ohio frontier was open again.

One year later government officials and Native American leaders met to sign the Treaty of Greenville. Under its terms, the Native Americans gave up their claims to all but a third of the Ohio Country. In return they received a few thousand dollars worth of trade goods each year.

With the signing of the treaty, flatboats filled with settlers once again swarmed down the Ohio River. Scores of new towns were founded, and the settlements already established began to grow. In 1796, Moses Cleaveland laid out a town where the Cuyahoga River meets Lake Erie. This town, named for its founder, would one day be Ohio's biggest city—although its name lost a letter somewhere along the way to become Cleveland.

Obstructed by trees fallen during a recent storm, Native Americans skirmish with American troops led by General "Mad Anthony" Wayne near present-day Toledo in the Battle of Fallen Timbers. The Americans were victorious and, for a time, the frontier was pacified.

In 1800, Congress organized the eastern part of the Northwest Territory as the Ohio Territory; the western remainder became the Indiana Territory. Two years later, the Ohio Territory's voting population passed the 60,000 mark—the number required for statehood. (At this time the voting population meant adult white males.) A territorial legislature met at the town of Chillicothe to draw up a state constitution, and on March 3, 1803, Ohio was admitted to the Union as the seventeenth state.

Tecumseh and the War of 1812

Ohio's population grew by nearly 200,000 people during its first decade of statehood.

In the early 1800s, however, it looked like British power and Native American resistance might halt the settlement of Ohio. Although Britain had been forced to accept American independence in the peace treaty that ended the Revolutionary War, the British kept several military posts inside the U.S. territory along the Great Lakes—a violation of the treaty.

From these forts, and from Canada, British officials and traders provided weapons to Native Americans and did everything they could to stir up resentment toward the young United States. Many Americans believed that Britain wanted to use the Native Americans as a buffer to keep the United States from expanding westward. There were other points of conflict between the United States and its former colonial ruler, but British influence in the Northwest was one of the leading causes of the War of 1812.

Most of the local Native American nations were happy to accept British aid and support Britain's policies. Unlike the land-hungry Americans push-

Several "utopian" religious groups settled in Ohio during the early 1800s, including the Shakers, so called because their worship included dancing, as shown in this print. One of the two major Shaker communities was in North Union; the area is now a prosperous Cleveland suburb known as Shaker Heights.

A missing eye, lost in a childhood accident, gave Tenskwatawa, Tecumseh's brother, a forbidding appearance in this painting by Charles Bird King.

ing across the Ohio frontier, the British were more interested in controlling trade than in settling the region. Thus, the British posed no threat to the Native Americans' homelands.

If the British provided the fuel for the fire that would soon blaze on the northwest frontier, two Native American leaders provided the spark: the Shawnee war chief Tecumseh, and his brother, the mystical Tenskwatawa, whom whites called "the Prophet."

An enemy of white settlers all his life, Tecumseh had fought against St. Clair and Wayne in the 1790s. But Tecumseh was not just a fighter: A

gifted speaker, statesman, and humanitarian, he journeyed across the continent in the early 1800s, seeking to unite all Native Americans in a confederacy to resist the advancing settlers.

Tenskwatawa, formerly a heavy alcohol drinker, experienced a life-changing vision in 1805. He stopped drinking and began to preach a new religion that urged Native Americans to reject the white world completely. After 1806, the brothers joined forces and attracted many supporters among the Native Americans of Ohio and the Indiana Territory.

Alarmed by the growing power and influence of the two men, an American force led by William Henry Harrison surrounded their village along the Tippecanoe River in present-day Indiana. Tecumseh, who was traveling among the Native Americans in the South, had warned his brother to avoid war with the whites until the Native Americans were united. Tenskwatawa, however, disregarded this warning and Harrison and his troops instigated a battle, during which they burned the village to the ground.

Britain and the United States went to war the following year, and Tecumseh led Britain's Indian allies along the Great Lakes. After helping the British capture Detroit and Moneguagon in present-day Michigan, a combined British-Indian force laid siege to Fort Meigs in Ohio, near modern-day Toledo. Twice the British and their allies stormed the fort;

twice the American defenders, led by William Henry Harrison, drove them back with heavy casualties. The British finally abandoned the siege.

In another siege at Fort Stephenson, 150 Americans commanded by Major George Croghan held off more than 1,000 British attackers. The victories at Fort Meigs and Fort Stephenson were bright spots in a conflict that saw several embarrassing American defeats on the northwest frontier.

The waters off Ohio were the scene of an important American naval victory in September 1813. At Put-In-Bay near Sandusky, a hastily built U.S. fleet commanded by Captain Oliver Hazard Perry defeated British warships in a hard-fought battle.

The Battle of Lake Erie opened the way for an American invasion of On-tario, Canada. There, on October 13, Tecumseh was killed fighting alongside the British in the Battle of the Thames.

The death of Tecumseh and the peace between Britain and the United States that came the following year brought to an end Native American resistance in Ohio. Even those Indian nations that had supported the Americans or remained neutral lost their remaining lands to white settlers over the next few decades.

With his flagship *Lawrence* battered and sinking, Captain Oliver Hazard Perry (with sword) is rowed to the warship *Niagara* to continue the fight during the Battle of Lake Erie. When the British finally surrendered, Perry sent a historic message to William Henry Harrison: "We have met the enemy and they are ours."

Settlers, Schools, and Slavery

At the time the War of 1812 began, about 230,000 people lived in Ohio; by 1820 that number had doubled to more than half a million, and by 1830 Ohio's population edged close to the million mark.

Most of the state's growth was in central and southern Ohio, especially in the Scioto River Valley. Thus, in 1816, the state government decided to move the capital from Chillicothe to Columbus, a newly laid-out town on the east bank of the Scioto River.

As in the territorial days, most of the people heading to Ohio in the early 1800s came from the New England states. There just wasn't enough fertile farmland in New England to support a fast-growing population. Also, the War of 1812 had sent the region's workshops and ports into a slump, and many people could not find work. For both single people and families, the Northwest—especially Ohio—promised a better life.

From Maine to Connecticut, "Ohio fever" swept New England. On foot, on horseback, and in wagons, thousands of people made the six-week journey across New York and Pennsylvania to Pittsburgh. There most

This engraving shows a view of Columbus as it appeared a few years after the town became Ohio's capital. The building at right, built in 1814, housed the state legislature until 1857.

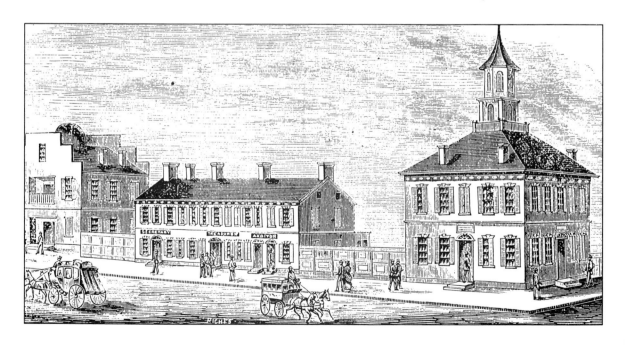

people traveled on flatboats down the Ohio River into Ohio itself.

The first stop for many pioneers was one of the busy government land offices. Here, the settler could buy neatly surveyed public (government) land cheaply—in 1820, for example, eighty acres could be had for $100. Many poor settlers, however, simply bypassed the land office, picked a plot of land, and began building a log cabin and clearing ground for planting. Usually, these "squatters" later got the chance to buy the land they had settled on before it went on the open market—a process called preemption.

But New Englanders were not the only Americans heading west to Ohio in these years. The "Ohio fever" touched other parts of the country too, and as different groups migrated into Ohio they brought with them the accents, religions, and cultures of their homelands.

Pennsylvanians and New Jerseyans arrived in the Seven Ranges area around Steubenville. Some were German-speaking, and many belonged to religious groups like the Quakers, the Mennonites, and the Amish, a community known as the "plain people" because of their simple lifestyle, whose many descendants still thrive in Holmes and Geauga counties.

In addition, many groups of settlers moved directly from Europe to Ohio. One of these groups, the Society of Separatists of Zoar, established a com-

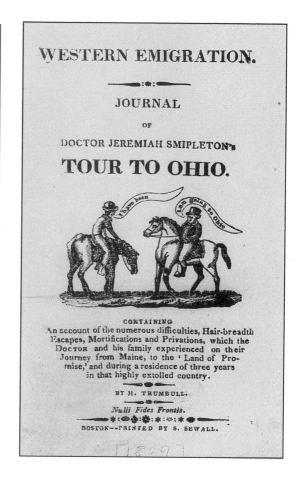

So many families left New England for Ohio that some New England leaders, fearing the loss of entire towns, circulated books and pamphlets exaggerating the dangers and hardships of life on the Ohio frontier. This 1819 publication informed readers that, among other things, Ohioans "walk on all fours."

munal colony in Tuscarawas County, Ohio, in 1819. British and American Quakers helped the Zoars, who were fleeing religious persecution in Germany, buy a piece of fertile land and set up farms, mills, and workshops to be shared by all members of the com-

Settling Ohio's wilderness often meant hard work for entire families. In this engraving, settlers clear the land of trees in order to make room for a log cabin and planting fields. (Many new arrivals avoided the treeless prairie because they mistakenly thought that the land was infertile.)

munity. At its peak, the society had 500 members and property worth nearly $1.5 million.

The Scioto River Valley was the destination of many settlers from Virginia, while Kentuckians spread throughout the southwestern part of the state. The arrival of so many Kentuckians and Virginians gave these parts of Ohio a distinctly Southern flavor.

It was the culture of New England, however, that dominated Ohio during the first half of the 19th century. The New England settlers brought with them a dislike of slavery and a respect for education. In both areas—the movement for public education and the struggle against slavery—Ohioans played important roles.

Although the Northwest Ordinance had stated that "schools and the means of education shall forever be encouraged," the reality was different in the territorial era and in the first years of statehood. While some pioneer communities quickly built schools for their children and hired teachers, others could not or would not do so. "New settlers who had learned to read in the East," writes one state historian, "saw their children growing up illiterate in the Ohio wilderness."

A movement arose urging the state legislature to set up a system of public schools supported by property taxes. In 1825, the legislature passed such a law, and within twenty-five years there were more than 11,000 public schools in Ohio, ranging from one-room cabins in rural villages to some of the first modern high schools in Cincinnati and other cities.

Higher education also began to develop. By the early 1820s, the state legislature had chartered two colleges—Ohio University in Athens and Miami University in Oxford—besides Marietta College, founded in 1797 as Muskingum Academy.

Many religious groups established colleges of their own, starting with Kenyon College (1824), founded by the Episcopal Church, and Western Reserve University (1826), set up by Presbyterians. In 1833, the Congregational Church founded Oberlin College in the town of Oberlin.

Oberlin was destined to play an important part in Ohio's—and America's—history. At this time, colleges were almost completely closed to women, but Oberlin admitted female students, thus becoming the first co-educational college in the United States. Upon founding, one of its stated objectives was to elevate "the female character, by bringing within reach of the misjudged and neglected sex all the instructive privileges which have hitherto unreasonably distinguished the leading sex from theirs." (Even so, Oberlin's female students were expected to wash the the clothes of the male students, clean their rooms, and serve their meals.)

In addition, in an era when very few African Americans could get any education at all, Oberlin went out of its way to recruit African-American students.

Many of Oberlin's professors and graduates—among them Lucy Stone, a leading advocate of women's rights, and Antoinette Louise Brown, the first female minister in the United States—were active in the abolitionist movement (the struggle to outlaw slavery). So many worked for this cause that one historian calls Oberlin "the town that started the Civil War."

Transportation, Trade, and Politics

If you had traveled along the Ohio frontier in the first decades of the 19th century, you would have heard everywhere the steady ring of axes felling trees. Across the state, farm families quickly turned the once boundless forests into countless acres of corn, wheat, and other crops. The region's fertile soil and the settlers' hard work turned the Ohio wilderness into a storehouse of agricultural wealth. In 1839, for example, Ohio harvested more wheat than any other state.

As pioneer villages turned into towns and then into cities, the first stirrings of industry began. Factories and workshops, the foundation of Ohio's mighty industrial economy, began to spring up. As early as 1819, a visitor to Cincinnati reported that "The manufactories [factories] of this new place . . . are extensive. An iron foundry, two breweries, several distilleries, a woolen manufactory, a cotton-mill, an oil-mill, a glass-house, and a white lead factory, seem to be the principal ones."

But the new state's growing economy faced an obstacle. Most of the food and goods produced in Ohio had to be sold and used within the state's borders, because it was hard to transport bulky grain and other products across the Appalachian Mountains to markets in the Eastern cities.

John Casper Wild painted this view of Cincinnati's waterfront in 1835. Besides flourishing as a transportation hub and trade center, 19th-century Cincinnati had a thriving shipbuilding industry—thirty-six steamboats were built in the city's shipyards in 1836.

Advances in transportation changed this situation and moved Ohio's economy into high gear. The first important advance was the steamboat. The arrival of steamboats allowed Ohio to use its great waterways—especially Lake Erie and the Ohio River—as highways for commerce with the rest of North America and eventually the world.

Steam transportation on the Ohio River began in 1811, when the steamboat *Orleans* chugged its way from Pittsburgh, Pennsylvania, to New Orleans and back again. Steamboats were vital to opening the Ohio River to commerce, because without steam power it was nearly impossible for vessels to fight the heavy current on the upriver part of the journey.

Seven years after that voyage, the steamboat *Walk-in-the-Water* appeared on Lake Erie. Plying a regular route between Buffalo, New York, and Detroit, Michigan, the *Walk-in-the-Water* and its successors turned lakeside towns like Cleveland and Sandusky into prosperous ports.

Land transportation, too, developed during this time. Zane's Trace, originally built in 1796–97 by Ebenezer Zane to connect Wheeling, West Virginia, with Maysville, Kentucky, was Ohio's first important road—although in the beginning it was little more than a path through the forest until it was widened and improved in the 1820s.

In 1825, however, the National Road, which began in Maryland, reached the Ohio border. For the next thirteen years the road was extended across Ohio, and in 1840 it reached its final destination in Illinois. Now part of Interstate 70, the National Road did much to tie together the new midwestern states, including Ohio, and connect them with the East.

The 1825 completion of the Erie Canal in New York State gave another boost to Ohio's economy. This waterway connected the Great Lakes with the port of New York, opening up the heart of North America to world trade and dramatically cutting the time and cost needed to bring Ohio's goods to market.

Ohio's government and businesspeople were quick to see the benefits canals could bring. Between 1827 and 1847 many canals were dug across the state. The Ohio and Erie Canal (completed in 1832) connected the great river and the great lake; another north-south canal, the Miami and Erie, was dug between 1843 and 1845 to link Toledo and Cincinnati.

Soon, however, a new and more efficient means of transportation—the railroad—came on the scene. Ohio got its first railroad, the Erie and Kalamazoo, in 1836, and twelve years later a line connected Dayton and Sandusky. By the end of the 1850s, steel rails had spread throughout the state.

This Lake Shore Railroad poster (right) advertises four passenger trains daily from Buffalo, New York, to Cleveland, Columbus, Cincinnati, and Toledo. At the peak of "railroad fever" there were seventy-six railroads running through Ohio to the South and West, or directly to the state's major cities.

Cincinnati's slaughterhouses were processing almost a half-million hogs per year by the mid-1850s. This lithograph (below) shows the stages the hog went through on its way to market, from butchering to packing. (One slaughterhouse owner called the pork-packing process a "disassembly line.")

'LOG CABIN ANECDOTES.'

This souvenir from the boisterous presidential campaign of 1840 shows the exploits of William Henry Harrison—some real, some exaggerated, and some completely imaginary.

Of all Ohio's cities, Cincinnati benefited the most from the revolution in transportation and industry that swept the state in the first half of the 1800s. Known as both the "Queen City of the West" (for its importance as a manufacturing and shipping center) and "Porkopolis" (for the huge quantities of pork packed in and shipped from the city), Cincinnati grew into the third-largest city in the United States by mid-century.

In 1840, the victor of the Battle of Tippecanoe, William Henry Harrison, was elected president—the first of eight Ohioans (although Harrison wasn't actually born in Ohio) to reach the White House. Harrison's supporters in the Whig Party worked hard to sell their candidate to the American public as a simple Ohio farmer who liked nothing more than to sit outside his log cabin with a cup of hard cider in hand. (Actually, the Virginia-born Harrison lived on a fine estate in South Bend.)

At campaign rallies across the country, Harrison's supporters paraded log-cabin floats made of buckeye logs and handed out countless souvenirs made of buckeye wood. Besides electing Harrison, the boisterous campaign established Ohio's state nickname—the Buckeye State. Harrison's presidency, unfortunately, was the shortest on record. He fell ill after his inauguration and died barely a month after taking office.

PART TWO

THE BUCKEYE STATE

The nighttime skyline of Cincinnati, Ohio's third-largest city, casts a colorful reflection on the Ohio River. In the foreground is Riverfront Stadium, home of the Cincinnati Reds baseball team and the Cincinnati Bengals football team.

While Ohio soil escaped much of the fighting of the Civil War, the largely antislavery state contributed much to the Union cause in both soldiers and supplies. Following the war, the state's industries continued to expand with labor provided by waves of immigrants from overseas. From the early 20th century onward, Ohio experienced great prosperity and population growth, interrupted only by the Depression decade of the 1930s. Starting in the 1960s and throughout the 1970s, however, Ohio experienced a severe economic slump, the decline of its cities, and growing environmental problems. In recent years, Ohio has made remarkable progress in improving life for its citizens and preparing to meet the challenges of an uncertain future.

Ohio and the Civil War

Like the nation as a whole, Ohio was increasingly divided over the slavery issue in the years before the Civil War. Many Ohioans with roots in the South (especially those living in the counties bordering the Ohio River) had no particular problem with slavery. But other Ohioans, especially those of New England background, hated slavery.

Among these people were the "conductors" of the Underground Railroad—the network of abolitionist Ohioans who smuggled escaped slaves across the state to Lake Erie and, finally, to freedom in Canada. Traffic on the Underground Railroad rose after 1850, when a stricter federal Fugitive Slave Law went into effect. The Fugitive Slave Law, part of the Compromise of 1850 (a set of laws aimed at keeping the peace between North and South), called for local authorities to help slavecatchers seize escaped slaves and return them to their masters.

Antislavery Ohioans resisted, sometimes with force, what they called "the kidnap law." In 1859, for example, the townspeople of Oberlin rescued a captured slave being held in the Cuyahoga County jail. Thirty-seven people were brought to trial for helping in the rescue, but a jury refused to convict them of any serious charges.

One of Ohio's most prominent abolitionists was Harriet Beecher Stowe. A native of Connecticut, she moved to Cincinnati in 1832 with her father and sister. Appalled by the reality of slavery across the Ohio River in Kentucky, she poured her antislavery feelings into a hugely popular novel, *Uncle Tom's Cabin*, which was published in 1852. It is the story of Uncle Tom, a good-hearted slave who is beaten to death for refusing to reveal the hiding place of two escaped slaves. More than any abolitionist speech or pamphlet, Stowe's book fueled outrage over slavery throughout the North.

The final break between the free and slave states came when Abraham Lincoln was elected president in 1860. Southern states started withdrawing from the Union to form the Confederate States of America, and in April 1861, the split between North and South exploded into civil war.

President Lincoln called on Ohio's governor, William Tod, to enlist 15,000 volunteers for service in the Union (federal) Army. So many Ohio men flocked to recruiting offices that

Besides its phenomenal success as a novel, Harriet Beecher Stowe's *Uncle Tom's Cabin* enjoyed long popularity as a stage play. Shown here (opposite, top) is a poster advertising one production.

In this photograph (right), a group of triumphant abolitionists known as the Oberlin Rescuers pose outside the Cuyahoga County jail, from which they had rescued a fugitive slave.

the governor sent twice that number of troops to Washington. They were the first of about 350,000 Ohioans to serve the Union cause, and of those nearly 34,000 died during the war.

Ohio's farms and factories contributed vital supplies to the Union cause, and the state's closeness to the fighting in the South made it an important base. Ohio also provided the Union military with three of its greatest generals: Ulysses S. Grant, who rose to become the Union commander in chief in 1864, was a Point

In this Northern cartoon from the Civil War, a female figure representing the Union prepares to slay a Copperhead—a pun, because the term referred to both a poisonous species of snake and a Northerner who favored making peace with the South.

Pleasant native; William Tecumseh Sherman, leader of the famous March to the Sea across Georgia, grew up in Lancaster; and Philip Sheridan, commander of the Union cavalry, was from Somerset.

No major battles were fought on Ohio soil, but the state didn't escape the ravages of war. In 1863, Confederate general John Hunt Morgan led 2,000 cavalrymen on a raid through southern Ohio. Hastily assembled Union troops kept Morgan out of Cincinnati, but the Confederates ravaged fifty towns before Morgan was captured at Salineville.

While most Ohioans faithfully supported Lincoln and the war effort, a growing minority began to call for peace with the South—especially as the conflict dragged on and the casualty lists grew ever longer. These Peace Democrats, or "Copperheads" (from the copper pennies they wore on their lapels) were especially strong in the southern counties. Their leader was Clement Vallandigham, a former congressman.

Vallandigham's antiwar activities led to his arrest by Union troops, and in 1863 President Lincoln "banished" him to the Confederacy. Vallandigham, however, traveled to Canada and from there campaigned for Ohio's governorship in 1864. The Union observed the election anxiously, because it was seen as a test of support for Lincoln and the Union's resolve to defeat the South. Vallandigham was defeated.

Age of Industry, Time of Reform

In the half-century before the Civil War, Ohio had gone from a raw frontier state to the third-largest state in the Union and an important center of industry and agriculture. In the fifty years that followed the Confederacy's defeat in April 1865, Ohio's growth continued at an even more amazing pace.

Old industries like meatpacking and ironworking flourished. New industries like natural gas refining and steelmaking sprang up, helped once again by technological advances. Natural resources—especially oil and coal—were tapped to fuel this terrific industrial growth. Hundreds of thousands of immigrants from Germany, Italy, and Central and Eastern Europe poured into the state, providing the sweat and muscle that made Ohio one of America's greatest industrial states.

Smoke from factories, blast furnaces, and plants dimmed the skies over Cincinnati, Cleveland, Toledo, and the rest of Ohio's booming cities. Their citizens, noted an Eastern journalist in 1899, didn't seem to mind: "Smoke means business, business means money, and money is the principal thing."

But the prosperity that industry brought to Ohio was shared by only a small group of people. Ordinary working men and women endured backbreaking and sometimes dangerous work, low wages, and no job security or protection from the "busts" that sometimes interrupted Ohio's economic booms.

The harsh realities of the state's industrial economy were reflected in its politics. The decades following the Civil War were a time when corruption in government was common throughout the United States, and Ohio was no exception. Powerful business interests controlled the legislature, while many cities were in the grip of political "bosses" like George Cox, mayor of Cincinnati for twenty-five years, who grew wealthy while ignoring the needs of their communities.

Still, Ohio in these years produced some remarkable politicians, including James Garfield, William McKinley, and John Sherman, who accomplished much at both the state and national levels.

If one person summed up the hard-driving spirit of post-Civil War Ohio, it was John D. Rockefeller. Born in New York State in 1839, Rockefeller settled in Cincinnati with his family in 1853. In the 1860s, Rockefeller became interested in crude oil, which was starting to replace expensive whale oil as fuel for lighting lamps.

Rockefeller and some associates founded the Standard Oil Company of Ohio. Through shrewd and ruthless dealings, Standard Oil crushed or took over competing companies. By

1880, Rockefeller controlled the nation's oil industry.

In 1892, however, Congress found Rockefeller's Standard Oil Company guilty of being a trust—an illegal monopoly. It took seven years to break down the huge firm into smaller companies. Ironically, the antitrust law that dismantled Standard Oil was written by a fellow Ohioan—John Sherman, brother of the famous general and a U.S. senator for thirty-four years.

While Rockefeller and his fellow industrialists built up business empires, labor leaders struggled to win better treatment for workers. Cleveland was the site of one of the great landmarks of the labor movement in America—the founding of the American Federation of Labor (AFL), established in 1886 by Samuel Gompers and several prominent labor leaders. The AFL eventually became the nation's most important labor organization. Another major union, the United Mine Workers, was founded in Cleveland two years later.

John Davison Rockefeller (top), founder of the Standard Oil empire, stares coolly at the viewer in this portrait by John Singer Sargent. Following his death in 1937, Rockefeller was buried in Cleveland's Lakeview Cemetery.

This pro-labor poster (left) from the early 1900s is titled *The Bone and Sinew of America*. By the start of the 20th century, 956 trade unions, representing 123 occupations and with a membership totaling 79,884, had been organized in Ohio.

The number of Ohioans who achieved the nation's highest office was a source of pride for all the state's people during these years. In 1868, Ulysses S. Grant became Ohio's first native-born president. Grant's two terms, unfortunately, were marred by scandal.

In 1880, James Garfield, a Civil War veteran who had worked on Ohio's canals as a boy, was elected president; he was assassinated in 1881. Seven years later Benjamin Harrison, grandson of William Henry Harrison, served one term in the White House. Harrison, like Grant and Garfield, was a Republican.

Not long after Harrison left office, the national economy went into a deep slump. With unemployment and misery spreading throughout Ohio and the rest of the country, Ohioan Jacob S. Coxey organized an 1894 march of hundreds of jobless workers from his hometown of Massillon to Washington, D.C. "Coxey's Army" was broken up by the police when it reached the capital, but the march dramatized the plight of the unemployed and poor.

With the nation still in the depths of the depression, Ohio's Republican governor, William McKinley, won the Republican nomination in the presidential election of 1896. McKinley's campaign was financed and managed by Mark Hanna, a wealthy and powerful Cleveland businessman. Supporters of McKinley's opponent,

William Jennings Bryan, candidate of the Democratic and Populist parties, accused McKinley of being nothing more than Hanna's puppet.

McKinley won the election and proved to be far more independent in office than his critics had predicted. (To be sure, Hanna, a U.S. senator, still had much power in both Ohio and Washington.) As the economy climbed out of the depression,

Shown here is sheet music for a campaign song composed for the presidential election of 1896. Before winning the Republican nomination, William McKinley served in the House of Representatives (1877–83 and 1885–91) and as governor of Ohio (1892–96).

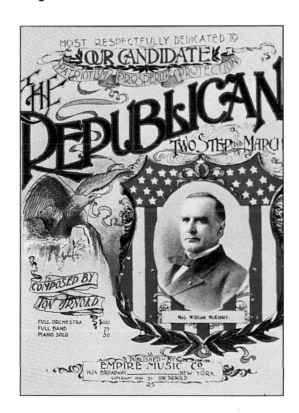

It was two Ohioans who ushered in the age of flight. After years of experimenting with gliders and engines, Dayton bicycle mechanics Orville and Wilbur Wright made the world's first powered flight in 1903 on the sand dunes at Kitty Hawk, North Carolina. This photograph shows Orville with his sister, Katherine, on one of the brothers' later-model airplanes.

McKinley again defeated Bryan in the election of 1900—only to die by an assassin's bullet in September 1901.

The beginning of the 20th century saw a renewed attempt to prohibit the sale of alcohol—an movement known as Prohibition—because many people felt that it posed a great threat to a stable family life. (The movement first began in the mid-19th century.) In 1900, the Anti-Saloon League of America (ASL) was organized in Ohio. Its main goal was to encourage people to vote against the sale of alcohol in saloons. They were successful— by 1910, fifty-eight out of Ohio's eighty-eight counties had voted to outlaw liquor, and by 1916, twenty-three out of forty-eight states had antisaloon laws.

Unfortunately, the Prohibition movement had a negative effect on the stuggle of Ohio's women for the right to vote. Because many of the people who wanted to ban alcohol were women, it was in the interest of the alcohol industry to prevent women from gaining the political influence that accompanies voting power. As a result, Ohio women weren't allowed to vote until 1919.

The first years of the new century also saw many reforms in Ohio's political life, as the ideals of the Progressive movement—which held that government should serve the people and not big business—found acceptance. Mayors Tom Loftin of Cleveland and Samuel Jones of Toledo, for example, cleaned up corrupt city governments and expanded services for poor and working people.

In the capital at Columbus, legislators passed laws aimed at fixing some of the worst abuses of the industrial system—like the Workmen's Compensation Law (1912), which required businesses to provide financial assistance to employees hurt on the job.

The election of 1912 saw another Ohio Republican, William Howard Taft, reach the White House. The jovial 300-pound Taft served a single term. Taft was later appointed chief justice of the United States—the only person to have held both posts.

In 1913 Ohio suffered its worst natural disaster to date. In April, unusually heavy rainfall swelled the Miami River; on the day after Easter the river flooded, sending a torrent of water through downtown Dayton. More than 400 people were killed, thousands more were made homeless, and property damage totaled a quarter of a billion dollars. A system of reservoirs was built along the Miami River in 1922 to control future flooding and to prevent a second disaster from happening.

A descendant of an early Cincinnati family, William Howard Taft served in several judicial posts and as governor-general of the Philippines (then an American colony) before being elected president in 1908. His Democratic opponent in that campaign was William Jennings Bryan, who had lost the two previous elections to another Ohioan, William McKinley.

Two World Wars

Ohio's population had passed the 4 million mark around 1900; two decades later the state was home to nearly 6 million people. Cleveland remained the state's biggest city, followed by Cincinnati, Toledo, and Columbus.

Many of the thousands of immigrants who came to Ohio in the late 1800s and early 1900s settled in Cleveland; by World War I three quarters of the city's people were either born overseas or were the children of immigrant parents.

Ohio's rubber industry began in 1870 when B. F. Goodrich moved a plant from New York to Akron. By the 1900s Ohio was the nation's leading rubber producer, with the industry concentrated in Akron. Shown here is a massive tire cast in a giant mold two-and-a-half stories high.

Ohio's fastest-growing community at this time was Akron. Thanks to the rubber industry, which came to the city in the form of the Firestone and Goodyear companies, Akron's population rose from 70,000 in 1910 to more than 200,000 in 1920.

Ohio's economy expanded even further in 1917, when America's entry into World War I boosted the demand for rubber, steel, airplanes, and motor vehicles—all made in Ohio—as well as grain and other farm products. The wartime boom also inspired thousands of African Americans to leave the rural south for factory jobs in Ohio's busy cities.

The war did bring trouble for the state's large German-American population. Ohioans of German birth or background were suspected—almost always wrongly—of disloyalty. Some lost jobs or were persecuted by local governments and "patriotic" citizen's groups. The town of Findlay, for example, fined citizens $25 for speaking German in public.

The postwar election of 1920 saw yet another Ohioan—Republican senator Warren Harding—win election to the White House. Promising a "return to normalcy," Harding served less than two years before illness took his life. The eighth and last (so far) Ohioan to become president, Harding was also the fourth Ohio president to die in office.

The 1920s was a generally prosperous decade for Ohio—but the good times ended suddenly in October 1929, when the New York Stock Exchange crash touched off a nationwide depression that lasted more than a decade.

Ohio's industrial workers were hard-hit; overall unemployment in the state stood at more than 37 percent in 1932, but conditions in some indus-

Newspaper editor, state senator, and unsuccessful candidate for Ohio's governorship in 1910, Warren Harding won the Republican nomination for president in 1920 as a "compromise candidate" and went on to defeat Democrat James M. Cox in the election. Harding's administration was tarnished by several scandals, although these didn't become public knowledge until after his death in August 1923.

tries and communities were even worse. By the middle of the decade, half of all factory workers were jobless, and at one point the unemployment rate in Toledo hit 80 percent.

Hungry and homeless families camped in parks in Cleveland and

Cincinnati, and even those workers lucky enough to keep their jobs endured deep wage cuts. Many of Ohio's farmers, who had suffered falling crop prices and land values even before the crash, also felt the pinch of poverty.

The state government began relief efforts in 1932, but there wasn't enough money in the treasury to do much. It took help from the federal government, in the form of President Franklin Roosevelt's New Deal programs, to relieve some of the misery that the Depression brought to Ohio.

Federal and state public-works projects put many jobless Ohioans back to work. The most ambitious project of the Depression years was the creation of the Muskingum Conservancy District. Completed in 1938, this $43 million program involved building dams and planting trees along the Muskingum River Valley to fight soil erosion and prevent flooding.

The Depression era also saw conflict between organized labor and business owners. In 1936, Akron was the site of a tense strike by rubber workers after the Goodyear Company announced plans to lay off thousands of employees. The strike ended with a compromise between workers and management.

A more violent strike took place a year later in Youngstown: nearly 50,000 steelworkers walked off the job when plant owners refused to recognize their union, the Congress of Industrial Organizations (CIO). Five people were killed and hundreds wounded in fights between strikers and company guards before Governor Martin Davey called in the National Guard to keep order.

The coming of World War II finally lifted Ohio and the rest of the nation from the depths of the Depression. Long-closed plants reopened to meet orders for defense goods; soon there was more than enough work for everyone in the state.

As in World War I, African Americans headed north to Ohio's cities, and by the end of the war they formed more than 6 percent of the state's population. Hundreds of thousands of white residents from the Appalachian regions of West Virginia, Kentucky, and Tennessee also migrated to Ohio during the war years. And with so many men in the military, the war brought new opportunities for Ohio's women. By the time peace came in September 1945, one out of every three workers in Ohio's defense industries was a woman.

The state's human contribution to the war effort was also tremendous. No fewer than 840,000 Ohio men and women—close to 10 percent of the state's population—served in the armed forces during World War II. More than 23,000 never returned home.

Police stand guard as steelworkers return to work after the 1937 "Little Steel" strike at Republic Steel in Cleveland (above). The strike began when the owners of several steel corporations refused to allow the Congress of Industrial Organizations (CIO) to organize workers in their plants. The owners finally recognized the CIO in 1941.

World War II opened up job opportunities for hundreds of thousands of Ohio women. Here (right), a female mechanic's assistant works with a Baltimore & Ohio Railroad mechanic on a train engine.

Postwar Prosperity

Ohio emerged from the World War II years with its economy restored and its population growing again. This time, growth came not from immigration but from the high birth rate that followed the war and by the ongoing migration of both whites and African Americans from the South. The state's population grew by more than 1,750,000 in the 1950s. By 1960, Ohio was home to almost 10 million people, making it the fourth most populous state.

The growth of cities, a longtime feature of Ohio life, continued in the post-World War II era. The Census of 1960 found that about three quarters of the state's people now lived in towns and cities, that only about 8 percent of the population were farmers, and that a million acres of farmland had been lost to development since World War II. Still, Ohio's productive farms accounted for an important share of the state's wealth.

In the years following World War II, the most important Ohioan on the national political scene was Robert Taft, son of President William Howard Taft, who was first elected to the Senate in 1938. A staunch conservative nick-

Completed in 1959, the St. Lawrence Seaway connected the Midwestern states to the Atlantic Ocean and allowed Ohio manufacturers and farmers to ship products to any port in the world. The seaway is 2,700 miles long.

named "Mr. Republican," Taft was a leading contender for his party's presidential nomination in 1952—until Dwight Eisenhower, the hugely popular World War II commander, entered the race.

As they had a century before, new developments in transportation and technology spurred Ohio's economy in the 1950s. In 1954, James Shocknessy organized the Ohio Turnpike Commission, which oversaw the swift construction of the Ohio Turnpike. This highway connected with similar turnpikes in Pennsylvania and Indiana to speed travelers and freight through the state. The road, later named in Shocknessy's honor, also tied into the great network of interstate highways constructed in the 1950s.

The 1959 opening of the St. Lawrence Seaway helped Ohio's shipping by solving a long-standing problem—big, oceangoing cargo ships couldn't pass from the Great Lakes into the St. Lawrence River and thus into the Atlantic Ocean. The seaway included a series of locks that lifted ships from Lake Erie into the St. Lawrence River. Thanks to the seaway, ships could now take on steel from Sandusky or car parts from Toledo and unload their cargoes at any port in the world.

The state also benefited from government spending on defense industries in the cold war decades after World War II—such as the expansion of Dayton's Wright-Patterson Air Force base into a huge aviation com-

A highly decorated Marine Corps fighter pilot in World War II and the Korean War, Ohioan John Glenn was selected as one of the first U.S. astronauts in 1959, and three years later orbited the Earth in the spaceship *Friendship 7*. Glenn was elected to the first of four terms as a U.S. senator from Ohio in 1974.

plex. Ohio entered the space age with the construction of an important National Aeronautics and Space Administration (NASA) facility, the Lewis Research Center, in Cleveland.

Some of the research done at the Lewis Center paid off in 1962 when astronaut John Glenn, a native of Cambridge, rocketed into space as the first American to orbit the Earth. In 1969, another Ohio astronaut, Neil Armstrong, became the first person to set foot on the moon's surface.

A Time of Protest and Change

The 1960s and 1970s were a time of challenges and changes for Ohio and its people. Although the state's economy remained healthy for much of the 1960s, Ohio's industrial expansion, which began before the Civil War, started to slow. The result was a slump—less dramatic than the Depression of the 1930s, but longer lasting and almost as damaging.

Heavy manufacturing and the processing of raw materials, which had long been the mainstays of the state's wealth, became less important to the national economy. People and businesses began to move from the "Rust Belt" of the Northeast and Great Lakes states—including Ohio—to the "Sun Belt" states of the Southwest, where the price of energy and the cost of living were lower. Much of this decline didn't take place until the 1970s, but even in the early 1960s, "warning signs were already visible," writes state historian George Knepper.

Ohio's economic woes were felt first, and hardest, in its cities. The decades following World War II saw rings of suburbs spring up around cities like Cleveland and Cincinnati. As middle-class people—and later businesses—left the cities for the suburbs, tax revenues fell and inner-city areas slid into decline. This left the citizens of Ohio's inner-city areas, including many African Americans, to cope with a lack of jobs, educational opportunities, high crime, and poor city services.

The decline of Ohio's cities began at a time when African Americans across the country were campaigning for civil rights. Ohio's African Americans—weary of city governments and police departments that treated them as second-class citizens—joined their voices to the growing chorus of protest.

Carl Stokes first ran for mayor of Cleveland in 1965, losing the election by only 2,000 votes. Victorious two years later, Stokes became the first African-American mayor of a large U.S. city. Stokes served as a municipal judge after leaving office in 1971.

The unrest in Ohio's cities boiled over into violence in June 1966, when rioting swept Cleveland's Hough neighborhood, leaving four people dead and entire blocks devastated.

The following year, Clevelanders elected Carl Stokes mayor, making the forty-year-old lawyer the first African American to govern a big U.S. city. Later, Carl's brother Louis was elected to the first of many terms in the House of Representatives. The arrival of the Stokes brothers on the Ohio political scene paved the way for other African-American judges, mayors, and elected officials throughout the state.

Although Carl Stokes did much to ease racial tensions in Cleveland, the city was again the scene of violence in July 1968, when seven people died in the "Glenville shootout"—a gun battle between police and African-American radicals.

Ohio's cities weren't the only areas in the state to experience unrest and violence in the 1960s. Many college students throughout the nation opposed America's growing involvement in the Vietnam War, and with more than fifty colleges and universities within its borders, Ohio's campuses were the scene of many protests.

The bloodiest and best known of these protests came on May 4, 1970, when National Guard troops at Kent State University fired into a crowd of antiwar marchers, killing four and injuring seven. The Kent State tragedy touched off a wave of protests and demonstrations on campuses across the country, and the words "Kent State" soon came to symbolize the deep divisions the war caused among the American people.

Ohio's economic troubles grew worse during the 1970s. With jobs harder and harder to come by in the state's declining industries, fewer people moved to Ohio and many moved away. The state's population growth rate in the 1970s was barely 1 percent. Cleveland alone lost nearly a quarter of its population between 1970 and 1980.

The state government felt the financial pinch, too. In the 19th century, Ohio had led the nation in the movement toward free public schooling; but in the 1970s, some schools were forced to shut their doors because of budget cuts. Perhaps the low point came in 1977, when Cleveland's city government declared it couldn't pay the interest on its bank loans.

Governor James Rhodes, who first served from 1963 until 1971, returned to office in 1975 promising to attract new jobs to the state. He offered generous tax cuts to businesses and took out newspaper ads featuring slogans like "Profit is not a dirty word in Ohio!" But Rhodes's campaign—his critics called it a "smokestack hunt"—was not particularly successful.

On top of its other problems, Ohio faced the environmental damage caused by decades of heavy industry. Smoke-belching plants had poisoned the air over many cities, and industrial waste and pollution choked many of the state's waterways. One incident in particular convinced many Ohioans to make environmental cleanup a major priority: In 1969, an oil-choked section of the Cuyahoga River actually caught fire and burned for days.

Throughout the 1970s, Ohio worked to clean up the worst of the pollution, especially in Lake Erie and along the strip of industrial cities that lines its shore. By the end of the decade, fish were returning to northern Ohio's lakes and rivers.

Slick with waste from chemical plants and oil refineries, the Cleveland Flats section of the Cuyahoga River caught fire in June 1969. The blaze, which raged out of control for several days, severely damaged two bridges (below)— and drew the nation's attention to the region's pollution problem.

Ohio Today

The story of Ohio in recent years is a story of hope and restoration. The problems of the 1960s and 1970s—poverty-stricken cities, economic slowdown, and environmental damage—are still problems, but Ohio's energetic citizens have done much to improve conditions in the present and prepare for the future.

Nowhere is this more true than in Cleveland. By the late 1970s, Ohio's largest city had become a nationwide symbol of urban decay. That changed in the early 1980s, thanks to the hard work and innovative thinking of the city's government and people.

A partnership between Cleveland's government and business put the city back on its financial feet by 1980; Mayor George Voinovich worked to increase ties between the city and its suburbs; and a citizen's cleanup program helped improve the environmental quality of the city and the surrounding area. In 1982, the National Chamber of Commerce gave Cleveland its All-American Cities Award to honor the city's efforts.

The nationwide economic slump of the early 1980s worsened conditions in Ohio—in 1982 the state jobless rate neared 12 percent. By the middle of the decade, however, the picture started to improve. Many new jobs were created, most of them in growing "service industries" like banking, tourism, real estate, and transportation, and in high-tech industries like electronics and telecommunications.

One Ohio success story of recent years involves the revival of Ohio's automobile industry. In the 1980s, the Japanese car manufacturer Honda built two car-assembly plants near Marysville. Honda's American experi-

Recipient of the 1982 All-American Cities Award, Cleveland underwent a massive construction boom in the early 1980s. It's now the site of numerous world banks and corporate headquarters, as wells as hotels, luxury apartments, and government buildings. The forty-six-story British Petroleum building, shown here, was completed in 1985.

ment proved so successful that U.S. auto companies, including General Motors, closely studied the plants' operations to make their own more efficient.

In the 1990s, Ohio dropped to seventh place among the states in population and to eighth in the value of its manufacturing industries. The state no longer wields the great influence it did for so much of its history.

But Ohio's strengths still outweigh its weaknesses. Ohio's central location and excellent transportation facilities make it a crossroads of commerce—a position it has enjoyed since the first steamboats chugged down the Ohio River. Within its borders lie areas of great natural beauty, and its towns and cities are filled with cultural and historical treasures; together these attractions draw growing numbers of visitors each year. Its many fine colleges and universities attract students from around the state, the country, and the world.

Back when Ohio neared statehood, its leaders chose the rising sun—symbol of hope for the future—as the chief symbol of the state seal. Close to two centuries later, it is still a fitting symbol for the Buckeye State.

Twenty-five percent of the state is covered by forest, and Ohio's nineteen state forests and one national forest attract thousands of nature-loving visitors each year. Shown here is a stretch of Ohio woodland, ablaze with autumn color.

Land area:
    41,330 square miles, of which 325 are inland water. Ranks 35th in size.

Major rivers:
    The Ohio; the Cuyahoga Grand; the Black; the Vermilion; the Huron; the Great Miami; the Little Miami; the Scioto; the Muskingum; the Maumee; the Sandusky; the Hocking; the Mahoning.

Highest point:
    Campbell Hill, 1,550 ft.

Major bodies of water:
    Lake Erie, of which 3,500 square miles is in Ohio; Grand Lake; and St. Mary.

Climate:
    Average January temperature: 28°F
    Average July temperature: 73°F

Population: 10,847,115 (1990)
Rank: 7th
> 1900: 4,157,545
> 1800: 45,000

Population of major cities (1990):

Columbus	632,945
Cleveland	505,616
Cincinnati	364,114
Toledo	332,943
Akron	223,019
Dayton	182,005
Youngstown	95,732

Ethnic breakdown by percentage:

White	87.1%
African American	10.6%
Hispanic	1.3%
Asian	0.8%
Native American	0.2%
Other	0.1%

Economy:
> Transportation equipment; machinery; fabricated metal products; petroleum and natural gas production; agriculture products (corn, wheat, soy beans, animal farming); and natural resources (coal, stone, clay, and salt).

State government:
> Legislature: Representatives in the 99-member House are elected to 2-year terms; senators in the 33-member Senate serve 4-year terms.
> Governor: The governor can serve two 4-year terms in succession, but must wait a term before running again.
> Judiciary: The state's highest court is the supreme court. There are many district, county, and municipal courts. In the judiciary branch, judges are elected for 6-year terms.

State capital: Columbus

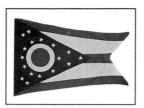

State Flag

Ohio's state flag is a pennant with three red and two white stripes. At the staff, a blue triangle containing seventeen white stars surrounds a white circle within which is a red disk.

State Seal

The circular seal depicts the sun peeping over distant hills, its rays extending toward a river in the middleground, and a field with two bushels of hay in the foreground.

State Motto

"With God, all things are possible." In 1958, a sixth-grade student in Cincinnati chose the quote from the Bible. His class petitioned the legislature and his suggestion became official in 1959.

State Nickname

Ohio's nickname is the "Buckeye State," after the buckeye, the official state tree. The state is also sometimes referred to as the "Mother of Modern Presidents."

Places

Adena State Memorial, Chillicothe

All American Soap Box Derby, Akron

Butler Institute of American Art, Youngstown

Campbell Mound State Memorial, Columbus

Clifton Mill, Clifton

Center of Science and Industry, Columbus

Cincinnati Art Museum, Cincinnati

Cincinnati Museum of Natural History, Cincinnati

Cleveland Children's Museum, Cleveland

Cleveland Museum of Art, Cleveland

Cleveland Museum of Natural History, Cleveland

Columbus Museum of Art, Columbus

Fallen Timbers State Memorial, Maumee

Flint Ridge State Memorial, Glenford

Fort Ancient State Memorial, Lebanon

Fort Meigs State Memorial, Perrysburg

Fort Recovery, Fort Recovery

Fort Stephenson Museum, Freemont

Gnadenhutten Memorial and Museum, Gnadenhutten

Harriet Beecher Stowe House, Cincinnati

Kelley's Island, Lake Erie

Kirtland Temple Historical Center, Kirtland

to See

McKinley Memorial, Canton

Moundbuilders State Memorial, Newark

National Road-Zane Grey Museum, Norwich

Neil A. Armstrong Air and Space Museum, Wapakoneta

Ohio Caverns, Bellefontaine

Ohio Historical Center, Columbus

Ohio River Museum, Marietta

Olentangy Indian Caverns, Delaware

Perry's Victory and International Peace Memorial, Put-in-Bay

Pro Football Hall of Fame, Canton

Rose Hill Museum, Bay Village

Serpent Mound State Memorial, Peebles

Sherman House, Lancaster

Taft Museum, Cincinnati

Thomas Edison Home, Milan

Toledo Museum of Art, Toledo

United States Air Force Museum, Dayton

Western Reserve Historical Society Museum, Cleveland

William Howard Taft National Historic Site, Cincinnati

Wright-Patterson Air Force Base, Dayton

State Flower

The scarlet carnation was the favorite flower of President William McKinley, an Ohioan, and was adopted as the state flower in his memory after he was assasinated while in office.

State Bird

The cardinal was made the state bird in 1933. It resides year round in Ohio and sings a unique melody. The male is colored a bright, beautiful red.

State Tree

Ohio's state tree is the buckeye, although there are few remaining in the state today. The distinctive Ohio buckeye leaf has five leaflets and greenish-yellow flowers.

Ohio History

200 BC–AD 500 The Hopewell Indians and other mound-building tribes inhabit the region

1670 French explorer Robert Cavelier, Sieur de La Salle, is believed to be the first European to explore the region

1685 American fur traders arrive in the region

1749 The Ohio Company receives a royal grant from Britain to settle and trade in the Ohio Valley

1749–51 Pierre-Joseph de Célèron asserts French claims to the area

1752 The Virginia Colony signs a treaty with the Delaware and Iroquois Indians gaining land south of the Ohio River

•The French overrun the English trading post of Pickawillany

1763 Following the French and Indian War, the Treaty of Paris gives the victorious British full title to territory

1788 Marietta, the first permanent settlement, is founded
•Cincinnati is established

1798 Cleveland is founded in the Western Reserve

1802 The Ohio Territory's Constitution is the first in the nation to forbid slavery

1803 Ohio becomes the 17th state

1813 Major George Croghan and his men fight off British attack at Fort Stephenson

American

1492 Christopher Columbus reaches the New World

1607 Jamestown (Virginia) founded by English colonists

1620 *Mayflower* arrives at Plymouth (Massachusetts)

1754–63 French and Indian War

1765 Parliament passes Stamp Act

1775–83 Revolutionary War

1776 Signing of the Declaration of Independence

1788–90 First congressional elections

1791 Bill of Rights added to U.S. Constitution

1803 Louisiana Purchase

1812–14 War of 1812

1820 Missouri Compromise

1836 Battle of the Alamo, Texas

1846–48 Mexican-American War

1849 California Gold Rush

1860 South Carolina secedes from Union

1861–65 Civil War

1862 Lincoln signs Homestead Act

1863 Emancipation Proclamation

1865 President Lincoln assassinated (April 14)

1865–77 Reconstruction in the South

1866 Civil Rights bill passed

1881 President James Garfield shot (July 2)

History

1896 First Ford automobile is made

1898–99 Spanish-American War

1901 President William McKinley is shot (Sept. 6)

1917 U.S. enters World War I

1922 Nineteenth Amendment passed, giving women the vote

1929 U.S. stock market crash; Great Depression begins

1933 Franklin D. Roosevelt becomes president; begins New Deal

1941 Japanese attack Pearl Harbor (Dec. 7); U.S. enters World War II

1945 U.S. drops atomic bomb on Hiroshima and Nagasaki; Japan surrenders, ending World War II

1963 President Kennedy assassinated (November 22)

1964 Civil Rights Act passed

1965–73 Vietnam War

1968 Martin Luther King, Jr., shot in Memphis (April 4)

1974 President Richard Nixon resigns because of Watergate scandal

1979–81 Hostage crisis in Iran: 52 Americans held captive for 444 days

1989 End of U.S.-Soviet cold war

1991 Gulf War

1993 U.S. signs North American Free Trade Agreement with Canada and Mexico

Ohio History

1816 The state capital is moved to Columbus

1825 The Erie Canal, linking Lake Erie to the Hudson River, is completed

1832 The Ohio and Erie Canal creates a shipping route between Ohio and the Atlantic Ocean

1841 Fighting in Cincinnati turns into a five-day riot

1863 Confederate troops led by General Morgan cause severe damage in southern Ohio

1869 Ulysses S. Grant is the first native-born Ohioan to become president of the United States

1906 Wilbur and Orville Wright, bicycle manufacturers from Dayton, patent the first successful aircraft

1908 A schoolhouse fire in Collinwood kills 175 children

1913 A five-day flood kills 467 people and leaves more than 200,000 homeless

1959 The St. Lawrence Seaway links the Great Lakes with the Atlantic Ocean, making it possible to ship goods from Ohio to ports worldwide

1970 Four students are killed when National Guardsmen fire on protestors during anti-war demonstrations at Kent State University

1995 The Rock and Roll Hall of Fame and Museum opens in Cleveland

Pontiac (1720–69) An Ottawa chief born in present-day northwestern Ohio, Pontiac led an alliance of tribes in an uprising against the British, known as Pontiac's Rebellion.

Tecumseh (1768–1813) Tecumseh, a Shawnee warrior chief, unsuccessfully attempted to organize a powerful Indian confederation to halt further white settlement in the Ohio Valley.

William Tecumseh Sherman (1820–91) Born in Lancaster, Sherman started a military school before joining the Union Army. He led the March to the Sea campaign that pillaged the Georgia countryside and led to the capture of Savannah.

Ulysses S. Grant (1822–85) A native of Point Pleasant, Grant was appointed commander of Union forces during the Civil War. After the war, Grant was elected president of the United States.

Rutherford B. Hayes (1822–93) Born in Delaware, Ohio, Hayes became the nineteenth president of the U.S. in 1876.

Ulysses S. Grant

James A. Garfield (1831–81) After serving seventeen years in the House of Representatives, Garfield, a native of Orange, was elected president in 1880. On July 2, 1881, he was shot by Charles J. Guiteau and died eleven weeks later.

Benjamin Harrison (1833–1901) In 1888, forty-seven years after his grandfather died in office, Harrison, a North Bend native, was elected as the United States' twenty-third president.

George Armstrong Custer (1839–76) Born in New Rumley, Custer led U.S. troops in a brutal massacre against a Cheyenne encampment in 1868. Eight years later, his entire force was killed at Little Bighorn, Montana.

William McKinley (1843–1901) A native of Niles, McKinley was elected twenty-fifth president of the U.S. in 1896. He was assassinated by Leon Czolgosz in September 1901.

Thomas Alva Edison (1847–1931) Born in Milan, Edison had only three months of education but patented 1,100 inventions in sixty years, including the phonograph and the electric light bulb.

William Howard Taft (1857–1930) A Cincinnati native, Taft became the twenty-seventh president of the U.S. in 1908. He was later appointed as a Supreme Court Justice.

Warren G. Harding (1865–1923) Born in Blooming Grove, Harding was editor of the *Marion Star* before being elected twenty-ninth president of the U.S. in 1920.

Ransom Eli Olds (1864–1950) A Geneva native, Olds was considered by many to be the father of the automobile industry.

Wilbur Wright (1867–1912), and Orville Wright (1871–1948) The Wright brothers manufactured bicycles in Dayton before they invented and flew the first successful self-propelled airplane in 1903.

Harvey Samuel Firestone (1868–1938) Born in Columbiana, Firestone formed the Firestone Tire & Rubber Company in 1900. By the late 1930s, his company was supplying 25 percent of the tires used in the United States.

Paul Laurence Dunbar (1872–1906) A Dayton native, Dunbar became an extremely popular writer of poems and novels about slave life on the plantations.

James Grover Thurber (1894–1961) Thurber, born in Columbus, was best known as a humorist and cartoonist. He was a longstanding contributor to *The New Yorker* magazine.

Clark Gable (1901–60) A Cadiz native, Gable was considered the king of Hollywood for nearly thirty years. He is most famous for his role as Rhett Butler in *Gone With The Wind*.

Bob Hope (b. 1903) Raised in Cleveland, Hope started his career as a vaudevillian actor and gained fame in the 1930s on radio and in films.

Arthur M. Schlesinger, Jr. (b. 1917) A native of Columbus, Schlesinger gained prominence as a historian and a winner of two Pulitzer Prizes.

John Hershel Glenn, Jr. (b. 1921) Born in Cambridge, Glenn is most renowned as the first American to orbit the earth in a spacecraft.

Paul Laurence Dunbar

Paul Newman (b. 1925) One of the most popular American actors since 1958, Newman has also had numerous successes writing, directing, and producing films. He is a native of Cleveland.

Carl Burton Stokes (b. 1927) Stokes was elected to the Ohio House of Representatives in 1962, and in 1967 he became the first black mayor of Cleveland.

Neil Armstrong (b. 1930) A Wapakoneta native, Armstrong became the first man to set foot on the moon, declaring, "That's one small step for [a] man, one giant leap for mankind."

Gloria Steinem (b. 1936) Steinem, born in Toledo, is an extremely well-known activist in the women's movement. In 1972, she founded *Ms.* magazine, which is published and edited by women.

Jack William Nicklaus (b. 1940) A native of Columbus, Jack Nicklaus was the first professional golfer to twice win all four major U.S. golf tournaments.

Steven Spielberg (b. 1947) Born in Cincinnati, Spielberg has directed a long list of highly successful movies, including *Jaws, E.T.,* and *Jurassic Park*.

Scott Hamilton (b. 1958) A Toledo native, Hamilton was a world-class figure skater in the 1980s. He won the gold medal at the 1984 Winter Olympics.

Pictures in this volume:

American Antiquarian Society: 25

Cincinnati Historical Society: 28-29

Cleveland Public Library Photograph Collection: 45 (top), 48, 50

Coverdale & Colpitt: 31 (top)

Dover Publications: 24, 26

Eastern National, Perry's Victory International Peace Memorial: 23

Hudson's Bay Company: 13

Library of Congress: 7, 10-11, 12, 15, 16, 18, 20, 21, 22, 31 (bottom), 32, 35 (top), 35 (bottom), 36, 39, 40, 41, 42 (top), 42 (bottom), 47, 60, 61

Media Projects Archive: 9, 14, 17

National Archives: 45 (bottom)

National Portrait Gallery, Smithsonian Institution: 38 (top), 43

Ohio Division of Travel and Tourism: 2 (Terry Cartwright), 33 (A. Miles), 51 (E. Turk), 52-53 (Terry Cartwright)

St. Lawrence Seaway Development Corporation: 46

Warshaw Collection of Business Americana, Archives Center, National Museum of American History, Smithsonian Institution: 38 (bottom)

About the author:

Charles A. Wills is a writer, editor, and consultant specializing in American history. He has written, edited, or contributed to more than thirty books, including many volumes in The Millbrook Press's American Albums from the Collections of the Library of Congress series. Wills lives in Dutchess County, New York.

Suggested reading:

Havighurst, Walter, *Ohio: A Bicentennial History*, W.W. Norton and Company, Inc., New York: 1976

Kirk, Dorothy, ed., *Ohio: The Heart of It All*, Modern Curriculum Press, Cleveland, OH: 1992

Knepper, George W., *Ohio and Its People*, Kent State University Press, Kent, OH: 1989

Roseboom, Eugene, *A History of Ohio*, Ohio Historical Society, Columbus, OH: 1973

Smith, Thomas H., ed., *An Ohio Reader: Reconstruction to the Present*, William B. Eerdmans Publishing Company, Grand Rapids, MI: 1975

For more information contact:

Ohio Division of Travel and Tourism
77 South High Street
29th Floor
Columbus, Ohio 43215
Tel: (614) 466-8844

The Western Reserve Historical Society
10825 East Boulevard
Cleveland, Ohio 44106
Tel: (216) 721-5722

INDEX

Page numbers in *italics* indicate illustrations